Living on the Cutting Edge

Living on the Cutting Edge

Dr. Christian Harfouche

Global Revival Distribution
Pensacola, Florida

Unless otherwise indicated, all scriptural quotations are from the King James Version of the Bible.

Living on the Cutting Edge
ISBN 0-9634451-0-3

Published by:
Global Revival Distribution
4317 North Palafox Street
Pensacola, FL 32505
www.globalrevival.com

Copyright © 1992 by Dr. Christian Harfouche
All rights reserved.
Reproduction of text in whole or in part without the express written consent by the author is not permitted and is unlawful according to the 1976 United States Copyright Act.

Third Printing September 2005

Cover design and book production by:
M.E.D.I.A. Group
421 North Palafox Street, Pensacola, FL 32501
Cover illustration is protected by the 1976 United States Copyright Act.
Copyright © 2004 by M.E.D.I.A. Group, Inc

Printed in the United States of America.

Contents

1. Walking With God..1
2. The Unexplored Territory......................................5
3. Fighting Your Battles Before They Manifest.......11
4. The Faith of Jesus..15
5. Perceiving Through Revelation...........................19
6. Going a Little Further..23
7. Spiritual Signals..27
8. Strength for the Battle...31
9. Mounting Up..35
10. Recharging Your Spiritual Batteries...................41
11. An Enemy Called Distraction.............................45
12. Empowered by God...49

Living on the Cutting Edge

Chapter 1
Walking With God

Someone once said regarding my life and ministry that I was the sort of person who climbed a tree, inched my way out to the end of the highest limb, turned around, and proceeded to saw it off!

I would venture to say that this depicts *living on the cutting edge*. I believe in getting out so far on the Word of God and on faith that only God is capable of sustaining my life and ministry.

Once and for all, we must make the decision that we do not need a formula; instead, we must follow the guidance of the Holy Spirit. We must learn that we cannot measure God in the balance of our human intellect.

Learning From Enoch

I want to relate the life of Enoch — his ministry, his personality, and the way he conducted himself — because Enoch definitely was a man who walked with God and lived on the cutting edge.

From this study of his life and ministry I believe we will be able to glean something that will cause us to live more victoriously in Christ.

We are going to focus on the spirit of a pioneer. Let's start by looking at Genesis 5:24, which reads, "And Enoch walked with God: and he was not, for God took him."

Zero in on that phrase "And Enoch walked with God." I want you to see something important here. This man Enoch lived in an hour of history when humans still vividly remembered the fall of man! Enoch's forefather Adam had bowed the knee to Satan and was cast out of the Garden of Eden.

Adam had walked with God. He'd had the privilege of sensing God's presence and hearing His voice as they fellowshipped in the cool of the day.

Living Under Judgment

But due to sin and rebellion, God excluded Adam and Eve from His garden. Angels and a flaming sword at the entrance forever barred their return to the garden and the resumption of their face-to-face communion with God.

Mankind were forced on a journey in life they had never experienced before. Women began to experience sorrow in childbearing, and men began to experience the weight and the burden of the unredeemed life, bowing their knee to the enemy that now ruled over them.

Adam was forced to work — to till the ground — but the ground wouldn't cooperate with him! It no longer bore fruit effortlessly; it wasn't yielded. Thus, hard labor was introduced into the life of man.

This was a desperate time for the human race. They were experiencing the judgment of having failed God. And they had only one hope — a futuristic promise that God had spoken in the Garden when He cursed the serpent:

> **And I will put enmity between thee and the woman, and between thy seed and her seed; it shall bruise thy head, and thou shalt bruise his heel.**
>
> **Genesis 3:15**

Now the human race could look forward to the coming of a Savior who would crush the head of the serpent (or enemy), but until then, they had to experience suffering, pain, problems, and the curse!

Enoch Walked With God

Out of nowhere, and in the midst of a curse-ruled consciousness, Enoch came onto the scene and, to everyone's surprise, claimed to be walking with God!

He lived in an age when his forefather Adam was still alive! Adam wasn't walking with God anymore, but here's Enoch claiming *he's* walking with God.

I'm sure his relatives didn't believe him. They probably said, "You're not walking with God. Don't you know humans can't walk with God anymore?"

There was no way under those conditions that fallen man could possibly be walking with God — *but Enoch was living on the cutting edge!*

Everyone said, "Wait a minute, Enoch. Don't you know we tried to use fig leaves to hide our nakedness, but it didn't work? God provided clothing for us by shedding the blood of innocent animals and using their skins for our clothing. Now we're covered, so God doesn't have to look at your wretched condition, Enoch!"

Enoch replied, "I don't know what you are talking about. I'm walking with God."

The Bible says, "And Enoch walked with God."

Enoch's relatives insisted, "You're *not* walking with God!"

Enoch maintained, "I *am* walking with God!"

They said, "You're crazy!"

He said, "No, I'm walking with God."

Enoch's Aggressive Relationship With God

Enoch did not have a passive relationship with God. He had an aggressive, forced relationship with the Lord.

This placed pressure on everyone alive at that time, because everyone was forced to look at the standard being portrayed by Enoch's relationship with God. They got offended by it. That's the truth!

They didn't pat Enoch on the back and congratulate him for walking with God. Instead, they probably were embarrassed by him and said something like, "Come on, Enoch, let's go talk to Adam. If anyone knows about God, it's Adam. He's the father of walking with God. Let's not talk about walking with God until we've talked to Adam."

So they probably took Enoch to Adam, and Adam said, "Son, you can't be walking with God. I walked with God once, but I'm not walking with God anymore."

Does that sound familiar? Does it sound like the modern Church, whose members can quote what happened in the past, but never produce anything in the present?

God is calling His Church to live on the cutting edge!

"You are not walking with God, Enoch," Adam said.

Enoch said, "Adam, with all due respect, I know who I am walking with."

Enoch did not retreat from his pioneering relationship with God — and he walked with God for more than 300 years!

Chapter 2
The Unexplored Territory

Enoch's walk with God was such an aggressive walk that it put pressure on everyone else. How do I know? The Book of Jude tells us what kind of man Enoch was and what kind of message he preached.

> **And Enoch also, the seventh from Adam, prophesied of these, saying, Behold, the Lord cometh with ten thousands of his saints,**
>
> **To execute judgment upon all, and to convince all that are ungodly among them of all their ungodly deeds which they have ungodly committed, and of all their hard speeches which ungodly sinners have spoken against him.**
>
> **Jude 14,15**

Notice something important that happened here: In the midst of a time when everyone was looking forward to the *first* coming of the Savior, Enoch looked all the way to the *second* coming! That's a pioneering spirit! *That's living on the cutting edge!*

"Behold, the Lord Cometh!"

Enoch said, "Behold, the Lord cometh." That means, "Look, I can see it!" (A pioneering spirit sees it as if it's right there!)

Thousands of years ago, this man Enoch not only walked with God but prophesied something that made everyone mad: "Behold, the Lord cometh!"

When you begin to prophesy things that are that aggressive, people will get mad! They will put up with you as long as you walk with God and mind your own business. However, when you begin to preach that God's judgment will fall if they don't line up with His Word, you'll soon learn what persecution is!

The Bible says that Enoch walked with God, "and he was not, for God took him." If we spiritualize that part of the text, it's significant to you and me living today — and it's prophetic for the Church of today, because the Church will also walk with God until it is not.

Paul's Walk With God

We are going to come to the same place in our walk with God that the Apostle Paul had reached when he wrote:

> **I am crucified with Christ: nevertheless I live; yet not I, but Christ liveth in me: and the life which I now live in the flesh I live by the faith of the Son of God, who loved me, and gave himself for me.**
>
> **Galatians 2:20**

Paul was so entwined with God, he didn't know who was who! That's why he said, "I am crucified with Christ: nevertheless I live; yet not I...."

If Christ is living in and through you, how aggressive is the Son of God? How certain? How pioneering? How authoritative? How sure?

Walking into the Spirit Realm

Jesus walked where there was no earth under His feet — just water! The Church will also come to that point eventually, because walking with God is not a passive thing.

Walking with God will lead you off this planet and into the Spirit realm, which is an endless dimension of unexplored territory.

Walking with God will take you to a place where revelation

knowledge has the capacity to reveal in one second many years of your future ministry and many months of divine orders and directions from God.

People come up to me all the time in prayer lines and say, "Pray for me. I need direction." They want me to give them an answer in the natural. They want me to say something definite like, "Do this" or "Do that." I just look at them and ask, "What's wrong with 'forward'?"

If you walk with God, you don't need direction. You know exactly where you're going!

When the Church Walks Into Its Calling

"And Enoch walked with God, and he was not, for God took him." Someday the Church of today will walk *out* of what it used to be and walk *into* what God has called it to be.

When this takes place, the Son of God will manifest Himself with overwhelming glory and power! The dead will be raised, amputated limbs will begin to grow back, and haters of the Gospel will be confounded.

No one will be able to deal with the unlimited potential and demonstration of power Jesus Christ is going to pour through His Church!

The Bible tells us that you and I have been buried with Christ by baptism (Romans 6;4). The Bible says that in reality old things are passed away, and all things are become new (2 Corinthians 5:17).

Since this is so, why do we attempt to take back into our *old* mentality the *new* thing God is leading us into? We weigh it to see if we will follow the new direction or not, even though we lost our right to make such decisions when we accepted the lordship of Jesus Christ. The only decision a believer has is "Yea and amen" to His commands.

Enoch's Testimony

Now let's look at another reference to Enoch:

By faith Enoch was translated that he should not see

death; and was not found, because God had translated him: for before his translation he had this testimony, that he pleased God.

Hebrews 11:5

This is a rich passage of Scripture. Notice the phrase "and was not found." This means the people looked for Enoch. If they really believed he wasn't walking with God, why did they worry about his disappearance?

What this passage means is that one day Enoch walked so far with God that God kept him! I believe Enoch had such a close relationship with God that he kept growing and growing and growing as God kept pouring revelations into Enoch's spirit.

Finally, one day God said, "Enoch, I don't have any more to share with you on that side. If you want to know more, come up hither!"

Enoch disappeared.

Someone asked, "Where's Enoch." People probably answered, "Oh, he's out walking with God!"

So a week went by, maybe two, maybe three, and the question arose again: "Where's Enoch?"

"Probably on one of his long walks."

But after awhile, when the voice that was offending everyone wasn't coming around anymore, they went out and searched for him, but he was not found. Enoch had walked right on into heaven!

The rewards of the pioneer are not only enjoyed on earth; they're also to be found in the heavenly realm. Enoch, by faith, managed to receive his own personal rapture! Don't you think a man like that is worth listening to? Anyone who can get his own personal rapture is all right!

Remember, the Bible says, "By faith Enoch was translated...for... he had this testimony, that he pleased God." See how aggressive walking with God is? Enoch wasn't only walking with God and prophesying judgment on the ungodly; he was saying, "I am pleasing God."

> And they overcame him [Satan] by the blood of the Lamb, and by the word of their testimony....
>
> Revelation 12:11

We often think "the word of their testimony" means someone getting up in church and shouting a little bit. No, "the word of testimony" is sharing the privileges of our relationship with Jesus to the fullest — unashamedly, like Paul did. Paul wasn't ashamed of the Gospel of Jesus Christ! Paul told the Christians at Corinth:

> My speech and my preaching was not with enticing words of man's wisdom, but in demonstration of the Spirit and of power.
>
> 1 Corinthians 2:4

That was a testimony!

The Bible says that Enoch had this testimony, "that he pleased God." If you want to meet someone the devil hates, find someone who pleases God. If you want to see someone who really defeats the devil, find someone who *knows* he or she is pleasing God.

Jesus said of His relationship with His Father, "...I do always those things that please him" (John 8:29). Standing in front of Lazarus' tomb, Jesus said, "Father, I thank thee that thou hast heard me. And I know that thou hearest me always..." (John 11:41,42).

What audacity! What boldness for a man to utter such words, that to the religious mind were found as blasphemy or pride. Pride, however, is not knowing where you are in God and not doing what you are called to do, hiding under the guise of false humility.

True humility is authoritative. That's the way Jesus was. When He said, "Father, I thank thee that..thou hearest me always," it was a humble statement.

You ask, "How do you figure that?"

Because there was a covenant — a relationship, an agreement, a contract — between the two parties.

But God will only do His part in such a contract. The Church, for example, is always trying to get God to do its part of the covenant as well as His.

If you should begin to be aggressive about fulfilling your part of the covenant, someone will be quick to criticize, "Well, you don't have to work it up!"

But the Scripture says to be instant in season and out of season. So don't be casual; be instant! Don't wait until the waters get stirred up to jump in; stir up the waters!

Be like Enoch: Every step he took was pleasing to God.

Chapter 3
Fighting Your Battles Before They Manifest

I'd like to share with you about fighting your battles before they manifest.

I believe in fighting the good fight of faith; not just for the sake of being in a fight all the time, but for the sake of glorifying Jesus in my life and seeing fruit come forth through my ministry.

I believe that many of us have gained a solid foundation through what we have learned in the past. However, unless we use it as a springboard to thrust us into deep waters, it could cause us to have a legalistic attitude which would keep us from expressing God in power and in glory.

What Next?

Most people fight their battles *as* they manifest, not *before* they manifest. For example, suddenly pain comes, sickness and disease attack, or a financial siege appears, all due to attacks of the enemy. When a Christian begins to see such things go wrong, he usually asks, "What's going to happen to me next?"

All of a sudden he feels thoroughly convinced it's time to pray. He makes a good confession of faith, calls a fast, and reads the Word. Why? He saw a circumstance.

The children of Israel served God that way: They walked not by faith, but by sight. Whenever they got in bondage, they prayed.

They failed to discern during times of weakness that their spirit man was hungering and thirsting, not getting enough nourishment.

Traps for Christians

There are two major traps Christians fall into. One is assuming they are strong; the other is thinking they are weak! We must learn how to discern our *spiritual* condition the same way we know how to discern our *natural* condition.

Because you and I, as natural people, have learned how to listen in the natural, we know when our body begins to feel something like hunger. For example, if we go two or three days without eating, we begin to feel our physical body weakening.

But how many of us have developed enough spiritually to learn the symptoms of when our spirit man is hungry and thirsty?

> **Howbeit when he, the spirit of truth, is come, he will guide you into all truth...and he will show you things to come.**
>
> **John 16:13**

Tuning Into the Spirit Realm

As a result of not discerning the condition of our spirit man, we are forced into fighting our spiritual battles when they manifest. Circumstances arise and *then* we fight the battle.

We say, "Brother, I want you to stand with me and pray. This is what is going on in my life..."

Those who haven't grown in the Lord yet will say, "God, don't You like me? Why is this happening to me?"

Have you ever prayed like that? Have you ever wondered what was going to go wrong next? I want to show you why we need to tune into the realm of the Spirit.

In a later chapter, we will look at a biblical account that will show how one man affected the whole world by properly perceiving what was coming. I will show you from God's Word how to fight your battles before they manifest.

At times I've been very sensitive to the tuggings of the Holy

Spirit. This is not a formula. However, normally when I begin to sense a dissatisfaction in my spirit, God is revealing to me that I need to break through a spiritual wall of restraint that the enemy is trying to keep me behind.

Often this is a signal about the movings of the Holy Spirit in my own personal life and ministry. It usually means that a promotion is coming!

When Dissatisfaction and Heaviness Come

When I begin to feel that the things I am doing in ministry cease to fully satisfy my spirit man, I recognize that wall of restriction attempting to keep me in a maintaining level, which is a casual level or a comfortable level. And this maintaining level is not *living on the cutting edge!* At these times, my wife and I begin to utilize every part of our spiritual makeup to discern how the Spirit of God is moving.

There are times when I perceive in the Spirit that there is heaviness in my spirit man. Heaviness can come through two sources.

First of all there are circumstances that can cause a spiritual condition of heaviness. For instance, when the devil speaks a lie; when a war, attack, or onslaught starts taking place; or when we experience other attacks from the enemy; these occurrences can cause heaviness to dwell in our spirit man.

When we're under these attacks, we need to stand against them and defeat them. We do this by standing on the Word of God and praying fervently.

> **For we wrestle not against flesh and blood, but against principalities, against powers, against the rulers of the darkness of this world, against spiritual wickedness in high places.**
>
> **Ephesians 6:12**

The second cause of heaviness is when the Spirit of God deals with us about a change in our life that has a price attached to it. It is in those times when many Christians fail God.

Chapter 4
The Faith of Jesus

In the 26th chapter of Matthew, we see where Jesus was preparing to go to the cross. Let's look at this passage to establish a background and a foundation for the things I want to share with you.

The only way Jesus could know Judas was going to betray him was through a word of knowledge. Actually, there was no guarantee that the traitor, who was out negotiating to sell his Master to the chief priests for thirty pieces of silver, was ever going to come back; no guarantee except the fact that Jesus knew by the Spirit that he would.

You see, what you know by the Holy Ghost must be more real to you than what you know naturally.

Did Jesus pick up and receive things from God in the same way the Church does today? Was He a man who operated under the anointing of the Holy Ghost? Didn't He make that realm available to all His children?

Of course He was a man who operated by the anointing! Furthermore, through His obedience, we can operate in the same manner today.

A Revelation of the Cross

Jesus had no guarantee that He would go to the cross. The only reason He knew He was going to the cross was because of revelation knowledge. The Holy Spirit spoke to Him. The Word of God showed Him:

> ...he that is hanged is accursed of God....
> **Deuteronomy 21:23**

Jesus knew that as the Messiah — the Redeemer, the One who would pay the price for the whole human race — He must hang on the instrument of the curse in order to save us.

Through the Word of God and the power of revelation, Jesus knew the only way to reverse the curse was for Him to give His life on that tree.

Until Jesus, no prophet had ever been crucified. In the past, the prophets were killed by stoning or other brutal means of death, but they weren't crucified. So there was no guarantee in the natural that Jesus' trial would result in His ending up in the Romans' hands and being crucified on a Roman cross.

Jesus walked in the perfect will of God and perceived what the Spirit of God was saying. When He laid His life on the line, it was not because of natural, earthly knowledge; it was because of what He had heard in the Spirit!

On the eve of His crucifixion, after celebrating the Passover, Jesus took His disciples to the Mount of Olives. When He began to share this knowledge with them, they had difficulty grasping the enormity of what He was saying.

Jesus' Greatest Fight

Next, He went to the Garden of Gethsemane to pray. It was there that Jesus fought — and won — the greatest battle of His life. He faced the greatest challenge any man could ever face.

You see, no one had ever been crucified, buried, *and* invaded the lower regions of the earth. No one had ever taken away the keys of death, hell, and the grave and then arisen in a glorified body without any blood in it, just flesh and bones.

Not only that; Jesus appeared again and then ascended on High with His own blood and sat at the right hand of Majesty. No one had ever done that!

A Sacrifice Made in Faith

As a matter of fact, if Jesus had not gone to the cross *in faith*, the sacrifice wouldn't have worked.

You may ask, "How do you know that?" Because the Bible says:

> **How much more shall the blood of Christ, who through the eternal Spirit, offered himself without spot to God, purge your conscience from dead works to serve the living God?**
>
> **Hebrews 9:14**

This says that Jesus offered Himself to God through the eternal Spirit. Anything we offer to God must be in faith. As you will remember, Abel's sacrifice was received by faith, and Cain's was rejected.

Therefore, for God to have treated Jesus differently, He would have had to break His own covenant — and God will not break His covenant.

Because Jesus went to the cross in faith, He represented you, me, and every person who will ever be born.

Jesus said, "It is finished!" Throughout eternity, those words will be valid!

The moment when He breathed His last breath represents the most powerful explosion of faith ever expressed in the heart of a man!

> **For there is one God, and one mediator between God and men, the man Christ Jesus.**
>
> **1 Timothy 2:5**

Glory to God, there is a remnant that has been purchased through the faith of one man.

Sorrow Is Not Sin

Now let's look once again at that scene at the Garden of

Gethsemane. Jesus tells His disciples:

> **My soul is exceeding sorrowful, even unto death: tarry ye here, and watch with me.**
> **Matthew 26:38**

Jesus was sorrowful! If a sorrowful soul is always sin, then Jesus sinned; but, of course, we know He did not sin. That means that having a sorrowful soul is *not* always sin.

There is a sorrow that comes from the devil, but there is also a sorrow that comes when the weight of the battle in the Spirit realm is heavy, when there is a decision to be made, when there is a breakthrough that must take place, when there is a call to intercession — when there is a call to your personal Gethsemane.

There is a summoning call in the Spirit saying to you, "A battle is coming! A battle is coming!" If you do not hear this call, you will not know what that battle is in your natural mind. But your soul will become sorrowful, because your spiritual antennae are picking up something and attempting to tell you that a confrontation is coming!

Chapter 5
Perceiving Through Revelation

We can fight our battles in the Spirit before they ever reach the natural realm because we walk by faith and not by sight.

I've been in my motel room at times and picked up conversations in the Spirit that didn't take place until two or three weeks later.

I didn't know the whole picture; all I knew was that there was a sound in my spirit that needed to be expressed; a spiritual churning that needed to come against that thing. And that spiritual churning was just as real to me as any symptom I've ever had in the natural realm.

The enemy was formulating a future strategy to hit me, but the Spirit of God was warning me, "Prepare yourself so when you get to that circumstance, you will already have won that spiritual battle."

In one circumstance the Lord warned me about, I could have told the individuals involved exactly what they were going to say. I already knew the strategy the enemy was going to use. Because I had been forewarned, I had the good shield of faith up, and I was able, through the wisdom of the Holy Ghost, to blast the devil away without blasting the individuals away.

> **For we wrestle not against flesh and blood, but against principalities, against powers, against the rulers of the darkness of this world, against spiritual wickedness in high places.**
>
> **Ephesians 6:12**

The Crucifixion: An Act of Faith

Jesus felt that churning, that sorrow, at Gethsemane. He felt the warfare that was coming against Him. Demonic forces were being lined up for the battle ahead. The enemy was planning his schemes against the Savior.

Jesus knew He was going to the cross, but if He was not strong enough when they came to get Him, He might have said no.

He later told the crowd:

> **Thinkest thou that I cannot now pray to my Father, and he shall presently give me more than twelve legions of angels?**
>
> **Matthew 26:53**

You see, Jesus was not a robot. He lived by faith from moment to moment, and He needed His inner man to be strong, His faith alive, and the totality of His being committed to what He was about to go through.

I know how much I love God and I know you love God, but if we were to examine our lives right now, would we allow ourselves through an act of faith to be crucified? That's a sobering thought, isn't it? And it would take more than a confession of faith to get a person through a crucifixion!

Spiritual Support

As we read, Jesus told His disciples, "My soul is exceeding sorrowful, even unto death: tarry ye here, and watch with me" (Matthew 26:38). In a time of warfare, when you begin to perceive the forces that are arrayed against you, it's not a sin or a sign of a lack of faith to ask strong people you rely on to stand and watch with you.

Jesus needed this kind of support on the eve of His crucifixion. He was just about to leave the people closest to Him, His closest earthly relationships. He was a man. He had emotions and attachments. He was getting ready to let go of the 33 years of His life on this earth to go somewhere He knew only through faith.

Jesus had never been in the grave. He had never been to the lower part of the earth. But the spirit of a cutting-edge person does not quit simply because he's never been there before. He presses forward, because he knows the guidance of the Holy Ghost.

A man or woman living on the cutting edge never quits!

Jesus was talking with God in the Garden of Gethsemane. Can't you imagine Him saying, "I don't know what it's like over there; all I know is that as long as the Spirit of God is leading Me, I will go through in victory."

Then the Bible says "he went a little further, and fell on his face, and prayed..." (v. 39).

How To React to Spiritual Weight

Let's stop right here. What does a pioneering spirit do when he feels spiritual weight?

I'll tell you what a casual Christian does. When you feel that sorrowful feeling in your heart, and you don't know what it is or why it's there, most of you eat!

Yes, you read it right: *You will eat even when you are not hungry because your senses tell you something needs to be done to fix that feeling you are having!*

Some of you sleep. "Oh, I'm so tired," you say — but there is no natural reason for you to be that tired. If you try to read the Bible, you doze off as soon as you open it.

It's not *natural* food you need or *natural* rest you need. Do you realize there are demonic forces trying to keep you from partaking of the right food — spiritual food?

The last thing you try is *entertainment*. You say, "Let's watch a movie or have some friends over for a get-together."

Running From Commitment

When you sense the symptoms of spiritual warfare, the natural man will tell you to do one of these three solutions. The natural man is trying to run from a greater commitment that God is calling the whole person to make.

Consciously, we may not know what we are running from, because we only know in part and prophesy in part. There are times when you will know, and there are times when you won't know exactly what you are facing in the Spirit realm but, thank God, the Holy Ghost knows!

In prayer we are led by the Spirit of God. When you make the right decision, all of a sudden that spiritual weight lifts. When you make a wrong decision, the Spirit of God will begin to give you a check in your spirit.

He will say, "It's wrong. Something is wrong. It's not right. Something is not right." You will begin to feel that sorrowful feeling.

Don't eat it away!

Don't sleep it away!

Don't entertain it away!

Pray and seek God only!

Chapter 6
Going a Little Further

Jesus came to a moment of decision. Verse 39 says "he went a little further." That is a pioneering spirit.

People say, "That's enough! Why do you have to be so *intense?*"

I reply, "No, it's not enough. I'm going to go a little further. Do you find this extreme? You haven't seen 'extreme' yet. Do you find this radical? You haven't seen 'radical' yet!"

There is a need for confrontation and aggression in the Spirit realm.

No one could look at the conditions in the United States — the drug addiction, the immorality, the fact that our children are walking away from God, and the rampant lawlessness — and honestly turn their hearts away from the obvious need for revival.

God's Summons

There is a summoning call from God, saying, "You can do something about the conditions of cities and nations if you will fight the right way."

Jesus went a little further. He fell on His face and prayed:

> **O my Father, if it be possible, let this cup pass from me: nevertheless not as I will, but as thou wilt.**
>
> **Matthew 26:39**

He went to find His disciples and found them asleep. The Bible tells us that they were sorrowful. Jesus had told them He was going to be betrayed and was going to the cross. He added, "According to your spiritual condition right now, when they come to take Me, all of you are going to forsake Me." (I put this in my own words, but this is what Jesus said.)

Peter said, "No way. I'm strong in the Lord and the power of His might. If all of them forsake You, I never will!"

Jesus said, "No, Peter. I perceive according to the spiritual condition of your inner man that you will deny Me before the cock crows."

God is no respecter of persons. God will never seal our destiny. If that were the case, then whoever was going to be saved and whoever was going to be damned would be damned.

The Flesh Is Weak

In the natural, according to his own perceptions, Peter said, "If they all leave You, I won't, even if I have to die with You!" Peter ignored the symptoms of the coming battle. He didn't gather strength from praying like Jesus did. He was weak.

Jesus went to the Garden of Gethsemane for strength. You ask, "How do you know that?" Another account tells us that an angel appeared to Him, strengthening Him (Luke 22:43). He needed strength. If Jesus had not gone to Gethsemane, I believe He would not have endured the cross.

When He returned to His disciples and found them asleep, He asked Peter:

What, could ye not watch with me one hour?

Watch and pray, that ye enter not into temptation: the spirit indeed is willing, but the flesh is weak.
Matthew 26:40,41

A Call to Commitment

Do you see what Jesus was trying to do with Peter? He was

saying, "Listen, what I prophesied to you is conditional. If you watch and pray, you will not enter into temptation." Why did He pick on Peter when He had ten more disciples, and He could have talked to any of them?

The reason is because Peter was the one who was going to deny Him. I believe that Jesus was thinking that the spiritual truths He had bestowed on Peter weren't strong enough to lead him into chambers of prayer and repentance.

What were Peter's spiritual symptoms? What was the confirmation that Peter needed to pray? His soul was sorrowful, just like Jesus' was. It was sorrowful because God was calling Peter to a commitment that cost something!

In Jesus' case, the cost was the cross. In Peter's case, who knows what it would have been if he had admitted to the crowd outside the high priest's palace, "Yes, I know Him. I am His disciple."

The Need for Fervent Prayer

Jesus said, "Watch and pray, that ye enter not into temptation: the spirit indeed is willing, but the flesh is weak." What does this mean? It means that you may be willing to please God spiritually, but in the middle of warfare, your physical body will begin to act weak if you allow it to.

That is why we need fervency in prayer. We read where Jesus prayed the second time:

> **O my Father, if this cup may not pass away from me, except I drink it, thy will be done.**
>
> **Matthew 26:42**

We read those words and think that's all Jesus said — that He casually prayed those few words — but the Word reveals there was much more to it than that!

Jesus Sweat Blood in Prayer

And being in an agony he prayed more earnestly: and his sweat was as it were great drops of blood falling down to the ground.
Luke 22:44

Jesus prayed until He sweat blood! The Bible doesn't record *everything* He said to His Father, but you do not sweat blood by casually saying a few words. No, *great drops of blood* came out of His pores!

Do you think that's aggressive and intense prayer? Have you ever sweat blood from praying? Jesus went a little further in prayer than all of us. Why? Because He needed strength. He was battling the principalities that were threatening Him. He was conquering the battle of the cross *before* it ever came.

Many of us deny the battle we are facing. We say, "Oh, dear, let's just forget prayer and watch television. We'll pray tomorrow." Not Jesus. He prayed prayers that are not recorded.

The Bible says that the Spirit Himself makes intercession for us with groanings that cannot be uttered. Why groanings? There is a need for intense prayer. If there wasn't, Jesus wouldn't have needed to sweat great drops of blood in prayer. His struggle was so intense, an angel appeared and strengthened Him.

Chapter 7
Spiritual Signals

Watch! In Matthew 46:43, Jesus found the disciples asleep again, for their eyes were heavy. That's a characteristic of warfare!

If we are not careful, we will miss the spiritual signals of God.

> **And he left them, and went away again, and prayed the third time, saying the same words.**
>
> **Then cometh he to his disciples. and saith unto them, Sleep on now, and take your rest: behold, the hour is at hand, and the Son of man is betrayed into the hands of sinners.**
>
> **Matthew 26:44,45**

Why did Jesus say, "Sleep on now"? Because there is a season to properly respond to the battle before it comes; but if we miss that season, we will find ourselves in the middle of a circumstance, reacting to the plan of the devil.

Jesus Was Ready

What happened when the armed mob came to get Jesus? What happened when Judas walked up and kissed Him? Jesus was not shocked. He knew it was going to happen. He had conquered it ahead of time!

Most of us would have been caught off guard and would have been hurt by this sudden attack that came like a fiery dart. We would have said, "I just knew it, but I didn't want to believe it."

Boom — Jesus' trusted friend betrayed Him! Judas kissed Him, but Jesus was ready. He said, "Judas, betrayest thou the Son of man with a kiss?" (Luke 22:48).

These words were so powerful that Judas went out and hung himself. Jesus had won that battle. Winning in the Spirit *before* the confrontation will keep your emotions flowing in the right realm during the confrontation.

When the mob came up to Him, He said, "Whom seek ye?" (John 18:4).

They said, "Jesus of Nazareth."

He said, "I am he" (v. 5).

Those words packed similar spiritual punch, for the men were knocked down by the power of God (v. 6). He had won that battle before it came, too.

Where would we be if Jesus hadn't received the strength He needed to become that final sacrifice for us?

Listening to the Invisible Realm

Jesus never turned His back on the tuggings of the Holy Spirit. He learned as a man anointed by the Spirit of God to listen to an invisible realm as His source of knowledge. Jesus was and still is the ultimate pioneer. He lived life on the cutting edge.

In the Garden of Gethsemane, Jesus ironed out every reservation, conquered every fear, and settled forever how far He was willing to go.

And when they came, Jesus said, "I am He." Those words, so thoroughly filled with commitment, were energized with glory! The power of God manifested and knocked the whole crowd down.

Peter picked up a sword. That's what we do when we haven't prayed through: We react rather than act. We try to figure out how to get out of the problem, so we pick up the sword of the flesh. Peter cut the high priest's servant's ear off, but Jesus was ready. He said, "Peter, put that sword down!"

Glory to God, Jesus had won that battle, too. Not only was He ready to go to the cross, but He was ready to forgive His opponents. He touched the man's ear and healed him (Luke 22:51). He was filled with glory!

Peter's Eternal Regret

After Jesus was taken away, His disciples dispersed. Peter waited outside the high priest's palace, warming his hands by a fire. Someone recognized him and yelled, "That's one of them!"

Peter said, "I don't know what you're talking about! I don't know Him!" And the third time Peter denied Him, he used profanity. Why? Because Peter fell asleep rather than pray. He didn't sweat in the Garden of Gethsemane, even though he had felt the weight of the coming battle.

People ask us, "Why do you have to get like that? Why are you praying so much?" Because a battle is coming between the Church and the devil!

Right now, you and I may not know *why* we are sensing the need to pray and be intense; but it is to receive enough strength so that when the confrontation comes, we will be ready to pick up the sword of the Spirit rather than the sword of the flesh.

All of the apostles will have to admit, if asked in eternity, that they went to sleep in Gethsemane. Peter will have to admit, although he is guiltless through the blood of Jesus, that he made this mistake. He denied the Lord because he did not yield to the summoning and the tuggings of the Holy Spirit when they came upon him.

Chapter 8
Strength for the Battle

The Bible says we're in the middle of a battle. We're engaged in warfare, and the weapons of our warfare are not carnal, but mighty.

When you are involved in warfare, you exert a lot of strength. You use a lot of energy. Sometimes you run out of strength, and you need to renew it. Have you ever reached a point where you were running on your own strength?

> **I had fainted, unless I had believed to see the goodness of the Lord in the land of the living.**
>
> **Wait on the Lord: be of good courage, and he shall strengthen thine heart: wait, I say, on the Lord.**
>
> **Psalm 27:13,14**

The Psalmist said, "I had fainted, unless I had believed …." Aren't you glad he said "unless"? Aren't you glad he didn't say, "I had fainted" and stopped right there? Today, the testimony of many Christians is, "I had fainted." They need to put the word "unless" in there.

The Psalmist didn't say, "I had fainted and have no direction and no hope, but God, in His divine omnipotence, reached down and helped me in spite of the fact that I was living in unbelief."

The Psalmist said, "I would have fainted — I would have lost strength, I would have fallen, I would have quit — unless I had believed."

"Ask What Ye Will"

We are a believing people. We believe in the living Savior — and we believe in answered prayer. We are not a people who just seek and never find. When we seek, we know we are going to find, because we know we have a God who said:

> **If ye abide in me, and my words abide in you, ye shall ask what ye will, and it shall be done unto you.**
>
> **John 15:7**

I'm not the kind of person who knocks just to knock; I *expect* the door to open! I don't pray just to talk; I *expect* an answer to come. I live on the cutting edge, *constantly receiving* from God.

The Scripture tells us that in the last days perilous times shall come. Do you know that the pioneering Christian, full of the Word of God and faith, operates in excellence in the middle of troubled times?

When the going gets rough, the Christian gets going. When the going gets hard, the Christian gets motivated, because our motivation is not the by-product of what we see with our natural eyes. Our motivation springs from an eternal source of strength who is secure in His Almightiness.

Security in the Word

Our security, steadfastness, and stability are based in the Word of the living God. "I had fainted, unless I had believed." Have you ever heard the term "just believe"? People will say, "Oh, just believe God." But what is it that we're to believe?

Notice the Psalmist didn't say, "I had fainted, unless I had believed I was going to heaven." You know you are going to heaven. However, just because you are going to heaven does not mean you are going to automatically live in victory down here! Many Christians are going to heaven, but they are being dragged there by the Godhead, angels, and other Christians!

Stepping Confidently Into Tomorrow

To live in victory down here means I've got to believe God's promises that belong to me while I'm living here on earth. I need promises that apply to the here and now.

God doesn't just promise us things in the by-and-by. I heard someone sing a song that said, "Yesterday's gone, dear Jesus, and tomorrow may never be mine." I don't know about you, but I'm *counting* on tomorrow! I have plans for tomorrow. I have plans for next year. Our ministry calendar includes next year.

This means that unless Jesus comes, there is nothing the devil or demons can do to stop me from stepping into my tomorrow and into the day after that, because God said to us:

> **With long life will I satisfy him, and show him my salvation.**
>
> **Psalm 91:6**

Are you counting on tomorrow? A cutting-edge Christian not only knows by the Spirit about his tomorrows; he lays hold on them!

The Psalmist said, "...unless I had believed to see the goodness of the Lord in the land of the living..." (Psalm 27:13). He was saying, "I would have lost strength; I would have given up; I would have faltered; I would have staggered at the promises of God; I would have fallen by the wayside, never to get up again; I would have backslid; I would have died — unless I had believed I am going to see the goodness of the Lord in the land of the living!"

When Faith Wavers

My answers are going to come while I still live. There is a weapon we know as time that the enemy uses against all believers. Have you ever prayed and believed, and a day later you still believed, and a week later you still believed, and a month later you still believed, and a year later you still believed, but as time went by, you began to waver and lose strength?

The enemy told you, "It's not going to happen. You're not praying according to the perfect will of God." He doesn't want you to have that thing you're praying for. He doesn't want you to receive it. He doesn't want you to see it.

If you begin to meditate on the devil's words, you will wonder whether or not it is God's best for you. You will wonder whether or not it is God's will for you.

Living in Eternity

The enemy uses the weapon of time with each believer under the sun. Time will weary you if you live under its influence. *Aren't you glad you live in eternity already?* Hallelujah!

Jesus said if you live and believe in Him, you shall never die.

That means even if your heart stops ticking, you keep on living.

That means you have *already* stepped out of time and into eternity.

That means you have already stepped out of the kingdom of darkness and into the kingdom of God's dear Son.

That means you have been taken out of the dominion of circumstances and all opposition of the enemy!

Chapter 9
Mounting Up

> **I had fainted, unless I had believed to see the goodness of the Lord in the land of the living.**
>
> **Psalm 27:13**

> **Surely goodness and mercy shall follow me all the days of my life: and I will dwell in the house of the Lord forever.**
>
> **Psalm 24:6**

When I pray and do not see an instant manifestation of what I asked for, the enemy comes and says, "See, it hasn't happened yet!"

My answer is, "Thank you, devil, for telling me that. That means I've got tomorrow to look forward to and the day after that to look forward to — because I know I'm going to be around until God fulfills His promises to me!"

If God said I'm going to be blessed, I'm going to be around until the blessing manifests. If God said I'm going to succeed, I'm going to be around until the success manifests. I believe I'm going to see the goodness of the Lord in the land of the living!

If you lay hold on something like that, you've laid hold on eternal life, and you've become an immovable person.

The Joy of the Lord

The Bible says the joy of the Lord is your strength, doesn't it? What is the joy of the Lord? It is "joy unspeakable and full of glory," in the words of the old hymn. Joy comes because of the absolute influence of spiritual truth.

When you have the joy of the Lord, it's because you believe God. You don't have the joy of the Lord because something good happened to you; you have it because Someone good lives in your heart. Good things happen to you because that Someone is with you.

When contrary things come your way, do not waver, because your joy is not based on circumstances; your joy is the joy of the Lord. Your joy comes as a result of hearing God.

When God speaks, His words are spirit and life:

> **For they are life unto those that find them, and health to all their flesh.**
>
> **Proverbs 4:22**

How To Live Through Shaky Times

The life of God — the *zoe* life of God — is your strength during turbulent times, shaky times, insecure times, and times when it seems as if God's promises are never going to come to pass.

However, as you hold onto God's *zoe* life and His promises, He will bring a renewal of strength and reassurance to you. You don't have to faint, and you don't have to fall. Once more, in the words of Psalm 27:14:

> **Wait on the Lord: be of good courage, and he shall strengthen thine heart: wait, I say, on the Lord.**

One reason why people faint in their Christian walk is because their heart becomes weak, spiritually speaking. That's why the Bible says, "Guard your heart."

The Scripture doesn't say God will guard your heart, the angels will guard your heart, or your wife will guard your heart. It says to guard your own heart! Guard it with all diligence, not with slothfulness, and not with laziness concerning spiritual matters.

Guard Your Spiritual Treasures

Make sure that you guard your heart as well as all the treasures God has deposited in you through the New Birth, the Word of God, the baptism in the Holy Spirit, and the gifts and the fruit of the Spirit.

You must *will* this effort; you must make the choice to guard these treasures. You need to say, "I am not going to let one bit of that treasure dissipate or leak out! I'm going to watch over it and keep it in my heart, because out of my own heart a well-spring of life will come forth.

Your faith will be tested as long as you live on this Earth. Many people who become weak and weary in their heart eventually faint and fall in their Christian walk.

You won't need to follow their example if you heed the following advice: When you lose strength, it's time to pray, mediate on the Word, quote the Scripture, think on positive things, pull down strongholds, and cast down imaginations!

Wings As Eagles

Hast thou not known? hast thou not heard, that the everlasting God, the Lord, the Creator of the ends of the earth, fainteth not, neither is weary? there is no searching of his understanding.

He giveth power to the faint; and to them that have no might he increaseth strength.

Even the youths shall faint and be weary, and the young men shall utterly fall:

But they that wait upon the Lord shall renew their strength; they shall mount up with wings as eagles; they shall run, and not be weary; and they shall walk, and not faint.

Isaiah 40:28-31

Notice that Isaiah gives us a description of God here! He tells us that God does not faint, nor does He become weary.

This passage also tells us there is no searching of His understanding. God does operate by deductive reasoning. He doesn't have to figure out a matter; He knows the problem before it is ever presented. He doesn't have to think about it.

Have you ever seen computers that are very fast at responding to commands and answering questions? God is not even like that. He knows the question, the prayer, the petition, or whatever *before* it is ever presented. He also knows all the mechanics that will have to fall into place to answer a prayer that hasn't even been asked yet. There's no searching of His understanding!

Your Understanding Isn't Good Enough

One reason why people faint and lose strength at some point in their Christian walk is because they are leaning on their own understanding. The Bible warns us:

> **Trust in the Lord with all thine heart; and lean not unto thine own understanding.**
>
> **Proverbs 3:5**

Why? Because when you ask God for something — when you're believing God's covenant and Word — it is imperative that you also believe He will fulfill it in His own way.

You should not try to figure out *how* God is going to answer your prayer.

Have you ever prayed for a financial breakthrough? Then have you recognized a certain natural source, and you said, "*That* must be the way God is going to answer my prayer!" Were you disappointed because that wasn't the way He answered the prayer?

When you put your hope in a certain way of fulfillment and it does not work out that way, you can become frustrated and lose strength.

For example, if you are believing God for a physical healing, if you're not careful, you'll say, "Well, I know exactly how to get my healing. I'm going to go to church Sunday morning, sit there in the pew, and believe that God is going to give pastor a word of knowledge. And when He does, I'm going to be instantly healed!"

You may put your faith out like that and God will honor it to a certain extent, but unless you're careful, you'll put your faith *in your own understanding* of how God will answer your prayer!

We must make sure we're not leaning to our own understanding. That way, if I come to a certain door in the natural and it doesn't open, I don't cast away the promises of God. I don't say, "Oh, God is not going to answer my prayer!"

Remain in Faith

Remain in faith. Know another door is ready to open. Know another breakthrough is getting ready to happen. Then your strength will be renewed, and you can continue to flow on with God.

Our God is a stable rock! He is immovable. He is certain and steadfast. If you center your life in Him, you will be stable and steadfast, and your strength will be renewed.

God gives strength to those who need it, we read in Isaiah 40. That same passage says the youth are going to faint and be weary. What does that mean?

In the world we live in, it doesn't matter how young you are. It doesn't matter how talented you are. It doesn't matter how intelligent or capable you are.

When you are living in perilous times in a troubled world — and when you are in the middle of a spiritual battle being waged by spiritual beings — you need more than youth, ability, talent, and your own strength — you need God's strength!

Chapter 10
Recharging Your Spiritual Batteries

Have you ever noticed how symptoms of hunger affect people? Some get grouchy. Others get snappy. Sometimes when you feel a little grouchy it dawns on you after a while, "I know what's wrong — I'm just hungry!" Then you eat, and everything's fine.

Physically you discerned symptoms of weakness. Your physical body was crying out for a renewal of strength, a new burst of energy, a meal that would give you enough strength to keep on going.

That same principle is true in the Spirit realm: There needs to be a continual spiritual refilling, a recharging and energizing of your spiritual batteries by the Holy Spirit in order for you to live a victorious Christian life. In fact, God has given us the blueprint of how to plug our recharger into the Holy Spirit.

It's not necessary for us to lose strength; we can continue to live on the mountaintops. God is the source of our strength. He recharges us and keeps us going in the Holy Spirit.

> **Even the youths shall faint and be weary, and the young men shall utterly fall:**

> **But they that wait upon the Lord shall renew their strength; they shall mount up with wings as eagles; they shall run, and not be weary; and they shall walk, and not faint.**
> **Isaiah 40:30,31**

It says the youth are going to faint and be weary. The young men are going to utterly fall. "But they that wait upon the Lord shall renew their strength."

The Scripture says that God sent His Word and healed them. The Scripture says that His words are spirit and life (John 6:63). The Scripture says that man does not live by bread alone, but by every word that proceeds out of the mouth of God.

Hearing From God

When you wait on the Lord — when you wait in His presence and minister to him — you will hear from Him.

When God speaks, He will give you a word that applies to your spirit man and strengthens it, recharges it, and prepares it to be an aggressor in life. That word will enable you to move on in the things of the Spirit and see victory manifested in your life.

Many of us approach the throne of God wanting a natural answer from Him. We ask, "God, what are You going to do about this situation? God, what are You going to do about this petition?"

God wants to speak to your inner man — your spirit. He is more concerned with your spiritual condition than He is with your natural condition! He is more concerned about where your strength lies and where your security is than He is about fixing things for you in the natural.

God knows if He can impart His strength to you, everything in the natural realm will bow its knee and line up. If God fixes everything for you and allows you to continue in a weak, mediocre condition, you'll soon walk through another valley, run into another problem, and ask God to bail you out of a dead-end condition.

God wants to put an end to your dead ends! I don't know about you, but I don't want to keep looking up to heaven and crying, "God, help me! I can't handle it anymore."

The Anointing Within

I'd rather stir up the anointing that is inside me. If I'm walking through a valley, I'm going to change it and make it an oasis. If I'm facing a mountain, I'm going to speak to it and see it move. If I'm facing an impossible condition, I'm going to blast it and see it destroyed.

I'm going to be strong in the Lord — how about you? Strong people can say, "Amen!" Strong people can say, "Hallelujah!" Some people are strong when God comes through, but weak when the situation does not line up with their own plans.

No weapon on planet Earth can stop a Bible-believing Christian! No devil is big enough to steal my testimony, take away my joy, eliminate my song, or stop my stride. Nothing on planet Earth can stop me from doing what God has called me to do!

I am strong in the Lord. I am strong in the power of His might. Greater is He that is in me than he that is in the world, for the Greater One lives on the inside of me.

I am thankful that Jesus rose from the dead. Most of all, I am thankful that He chose to make my body His temple. He refused to be a God who was far away. He moved so close that He moved inside of me!

There is a power on the inside of you that will fight your battles for you if you learn to rely on it and tap into it. It will blast your enemies for you. It will answer your prayers for you. It will illuminate your path for you.

It will cause you to walk on water, move mountains, raise the dead, open the ears of the deaf, and heal the blind. It will cause you to run the race and not be weary, and fight the fight and not lose.

Paul's Perseverance

Scripture says that when Paul had finished his journey, they beat him, but he kept on preaching. They stoned him, but he got up to preach again. He was shipwrecked, but he swam ashore. There, he was bitten by a snake, but he shook it into the fire and caused revival to come to that place!

The Roman Empire thought it had captured him, but Paul held

the whole Roman Empire captive.

When he wrote to Timothy that second time, he didn't say, "I am dying and I don't know what to do"; he said:

> **...the time of my departure is at hand.**
>
> **I have fought a good fight, I have finished my course, I have kept the faith.**
>
> 2 Timothy 4:6,7

People like Paul and Timothy are the kind of people who are going to rise up in this decade — people who live on the cutting edge, not weaklings who don't know how to fight the good fight of faith.

God is raising up Bible-believing Christians who can leap over a wall and run through a troop — people who know how to see God manifest in and through their lives.

Chapter 11
An Enemy Called Distraction

If you are fighting an enemy — and I know you are — your most challenging enemy is the enemy I call "distraction." He's been working on you hour after hour, day after day. He's been distracting you from what really counts.

Most of you think your job is what really counts, your mate is what really counts, your plans are what really counts, or the future is what really counts.

What really counts is that God put His Spirit inside you to make you a sign to all the heathen who live on planet Earth! He wants to parade you on this planet as an extension of Jesus Christ! He wants to walk you in the nations as a healer, an encourager, and a minister in your own right.

Each of you is a potential Enoch who can walk with God all the way, and each of you has been called to seek first God's kingdom and His righteousness.

God's Plan for Your Life

I want you to know you do not have a choice as to whether or not to respond to the promptings of the Holy Spirit. You simply do not have a choice in the matter! It is not a question; it is a *command* from God that says, "Go ye into all the world and make disciples of all nations."

Your priority — and the reason you live — is to bring God glory on planet Earth. You are an evangelist for God. Your mission is to go out and pull people into His kingdom.

I am persuaded that the reason Christians don't see their families saved is because they don't put their family under enough pressure. They don't believe strong enough to harass them with the Word of God and bombard them with prayer! You must continually invite them to church. You must keep bringing them to a place where the Holy Spirit is moving.

I guarantee you, when the church gets on fire for God, we will recognize God's priorities, and it will not be long before the world will be invaded and literally turned upside down for God.

Also, it will not be long before hospitals are emptied. Bible-believing Christians will march in there, lay hands on the terminally ill, and see them healed by the power of the living God. You are called to do that. You are chosen to do that.

Mounting Up With God's Strength

The Scripture says if you wait on the Lord, you will do certain things for Him. Let me tell you what you will *not* do for Him: You will not fall, faint, cry, weep, mourn, and groan. You will not wait without strength. But you *will* mount up with wings like eagles. You *will* run and not be weary, and walk and not faint.

Do you want the strength of God in your life? Do you want to know *why* the strength of God comes to you? There are three reasons why God's strength comes in your life, and one of them is to cause you to mount up.

Notice the Scripture says God's people shall mount up with wings as eagles; it doesn't say God will mount them up. Do you know you are not a puppet?

You are not the by-product of your circumstances or your environment. You should be the by-product of the Word of the living God. You are not a puppet on a string that God chooses to lift above the storm if He wants to and lower a little bit under the rain if He wants to.

Don't Settle for Chicken Wings!

No! You can choose which set of wings to travel with. If you want the wings of a chicken or a turkey, you can have them. Or, you can choose the wings of an eagle!

In other words, *you don't have to settle for second best in God.* When you wait on Him, you wait for His best, and you say, "God, I'm waiting in your presence. You said we could come boldly before the throne of grace to obtain mercy and find grace to help in the time of need, and I'm not leaving with any other wings except eagles' wings."

The strength of God comes to help you mount up, for eagles mount up above the storm. It is never said of eagles that they do not face storms, because eagles know how to handle storms!

When all the chickens run for shelter in the chicken coop, and all the other animals run away and hide from the storm, the eagle faces the storm! He locks his wings and flies upward, allowing the strength of the storm to carry him even farther up so he can enjoy the sunshine and the victory of ruling from far above the storm!

Face Your Storm

That's what the Bible-believing Christian is supposed to be like. The Scripture says that no weapon formed against me shall prosper. It says I'm not moved by what I see.

So the Christian faces the storm with complete confidence that he's got the strength to fly over it, not with the intention of going under it.

One of the reasons God's strength comes is to cause you to mount up. That means, if you don't *plan* to mount up, you won't get God's strength. That's why some people don't get their prayers answered. They pray, "God, take the storm away!"

Have you ever heard messages preached that said, "You know, Jesus can calm your storm for you. Jesus can move the mountain for you." But Jesus said if *you* tell the mountain to be removed, it will be.

When trouble comes, most Christians pray, "God, why is this happening to me? I'm a Christian. Don't You love me? Don't You see what I'm going through? Take the storm away! I can't handle another day!"

But Bible-believing people say, "God, I know there is a storm raging, and I know there is a strength that is stronger than the storm. Just give me the strength to rise above it."

I'm not afraid of a storm; I just want to be on the right side of it. I'm not afraid of the circumstances; I just want to be on top of them.

I don't want to be like Peter, who walks for a while, goes under, and needs a helping hand. Aren't you glad Jesus had mercy? When Peter yelled, "Help!" Jesus said, "I'll help you," and He brought him back into the boat. Thank God for mercy!

The first reason you receive spiritual strength in your life is to enable you to *mount up* above every circumstance. The second reason for renewing your strength is to enable you to *run* and not be weary. The third reason is for you to *walk* and not faint.

So if you want God's strength, you want it for three reasons: to mount up, to run, and to walk. Thank God, I know if I miss it, He'll come through — but I'm not looking for the "missing- it" part. I want to do the "mounting-up" part, the "running" part, and the "walking" part.

God doesn't give strength to you to sit. You don't need strength for that. No, the Bible says they shall renew their strength and they shall mount up, run, and walk!

Chapter 12
Empowered by God

When you run, there is the potential of becoming weary. However, when you run your race through the power of the Holy Spirit and God's igniting force of biblical revelation, you're not going to be weary. You're not going to falter and faint halfway through; you're going to renew your strength and make it to the finish line.

If you're running right now and you're weary, the answer is not to tell God to stop or to say, "Oh, dear, I've done all I can." No, the answer is to get more strength to run the race.

At worst, a Christian is walking. At best, he is mounting up on wings like an eagle. In mediocrity, he is still walking. Jesus said, "You will walk on scorpions and snakes." That's good enough, isn't it?

If I'm just walking, I'm walking on top. If I'm running, that's even better. But, ultimately, I can mount up with wings of eagles!

Don't Be Weary

The Scripture says in Galatians 6:9:

And let us not be weary in well doing: for in due season we shall reap, if we faint not.

Don't be weary in well-doing. Paul is talking about sowing and reaping. He's telling us to sow the Word, to sow to the Spirit, and to sow tithes and offerings into the kingdom of God.

Don't be weary in doing this, because there will come a season when you will *reap* what you sow. This means there is also a season when you just *sow*.

It's in the season of sowing that people get weary. They say, "I've done this, and I've done that, and I've done the other, and I can't do it anymore!" Paul tells us not to say that, but to ask for the strength to keep on sowing.

The Blessings of Standing Firm

If you don't faint — if the situation does not overwhelm you — God will intercept you on your way. All of a sudden "more than enough" will overflow your life, and success will manifest on your behalf.

Be not weary in well-doing! You're going to have to run faster, walk stronger, mount up with more commitment, give more, guard your heart more carefully, continue to think in line with the Word of God, and be more sober in your spiritual walk.

No one can do that for you. No one but you can determine what level of spiritual success you will walk in. I don't know about you, but I want to go to the top!

Put on the Whole Armor of God

Paul gave this advice to the believers at Ephesus:

> **Finally, my brethren, be strong in the Lord, and in the power of his might.**
>
> **Put on the whole armour of God, that ye may be able to stand against the wiles of the devil.**
>
> **For we wrestle not against flesh and blood, but against principalities, against powers, against the rulers of the darkness of this world, against spiritual wickedness in high places.**
>
> **Wherefore take unto you the whole armour of God, that ye may be able to withstand in the evil day, and having done**

> **all, to stand.**
>
> **Stand therefore....**
>
> Ephesians 6:10-14

In the previous chapter, we studied three reasons why the strength of God comes to help us. Now we see a fourth reason: to enable us to *stand*.

Sometimes all you can do is stand. You can't even walk, let alone run or mount up. Standing is good enough; it's better than sitting or lying down.

It pays to be strong in the Lord and in the power of His might. It pays to put on the whole armor of God. You need strength to stand.

The fact that you're standing means you're a prime candidate for more strength. You see, if I'm standing, it means I'm getting ready to walk; and if I'm walking, I'm getting ready to run; and if I'm running, I'm getting ready to mount up.

How To Get God's Blessings

And the Scripture says, "...having done all, to stand. Stand therefore...." Sometimes you have to do everything you know to do just to stand — but when you get in that standing position, watch out, devil! If you say, "I want God to bless me," then stand. Stand!

Some of us are sitting, and some of us are lying down, and we're asking, "God, why won't this thing I'm asking for happen in my life?"

Have you ever had your car in neutral? You know it doesn't matter how much you "put the pedal on the metal"; that car is going nowhere (unless it's heading downhill) if it's not in gear. But once you put it in the right gear, you don't need to give it much gas to get it going.

Have you ever seen the powerful, turbo-charged sports cars? Have you ever seen them driving next to some junkers? Driving through city streets at 35 miles per hour, from red light to red light, they all perform pretty much the same. It doesn't matter how good the sports car looks at 35 miles per hour; everything looks the same in a traffic jam.

The Stress Test

That's how we are when everything is going well for us. A spiritual giant and a babe in Christ will walk side by side, both praising God, and you can't tell which is which. (Even babies can "talk the talk.") They're happy, and they're beaming, "I love my wife, I love my job, everything's wonderful."

You begin to see the sports car excel when it gets into the hill country. Winding roads take it uphill, downhill, and around sharp turns. All of a sudden, certain features start to stand out: The tires have strong traction; the suspension is made for that kind of terrain; and the engine can handle the steep hills without going, "Putt, putt, putt."

You don't have to push it uphill and pump the brake all the way downhill. It zooms up and down hills and around curves, having the time of its life, while the junker has everything it can do to struggle up the first hill!

That's how we determine victory and maturity in the Lord. Here you are, a spiritual giant. You are strong in the Lord whenever things are going well. That's when you say, "I thank You, Lord, that greater is He that is in me than he that is in the world." The next thing you'll know, you'll have a group of people around you, patting you on the back and supporting you.

When We Reach Hill Country

But when you get to the hill country, where there are winding roads, and a storm threatens you in the foothills, all of a sudden the junkers begin to drop back.

But those who wait on the Lord shall renew their strength, and they will mount up with wings as eagles. They will run and not be weary, and they will walk and not faint!

Say out loud: "I'm going to stand; I'm going to walk; I'm going to run; and I'm going to mount up! I will not sit; I will not faint; I will not fail. I'm going on with God, and I'm going all the way." I'm going to live on the cutting edge.

Habakkuk 3:17-19 describes that mountainous terrain, that storm, and that battle for us:

> **Although the fig tree shall not blossom, neither shall fruit be in the vines; the labour of the olive tree shall fail, and the fields shall yield no meat; the flock shall be cut off from the fold, and there shall be no herd in the stalls:**
>
> **Yet I will rejoice in the Lord, I will joy in the God of my salvation.**
>
> **The Lord God is my strength, and he will make my feet like hinds' feet, and he will make me to walk upon mine high places.**

Those are miserable conditions described in verse 17! This farmer has a fig tree that's not blossoming, so God can't provide for him through it. He's got no fruit on his vines. He's got an olive tree, but its fruit is being aborted and falling off, so it's not bearing, either. His fields are not yielding their crops. His flock is gone, and there is no herd in the stalls.

"If You Just Had Enough Faith..."

This man had everything to look forward to, yet nothing was going right. Have you ever been in a circumstance like that, when the devil comes and says, "Well, if you just had enough faith, you wouldn't be where you are." That's a lie, because *where you are* does not matter; it's *where you are going* that matters!

Notice what this farmer said: "Although my trees are not bearing, my vines have nothing, my fields are empty, the flock is cut off, and the whole situation seems to be barren, yet I will rejoice in the Lord, and I will joy in the God of my salvation."

Why? Because "the Lord God is my strength, and he will make my feet like hinds' feet, and he will make me to walk upon mine high places."

Notice what this man *didn't* say: "Oh, you know, everything's going bad. The Lord giveth and the Lord taketh away." Aren't you glad he didn't say that? Aren't you glad he didn't say, "Everything is miserable, bless His holy Name!"

Living on the Cutting Edge

What he *did* say was: "The reason I am not moved by any of these conditions is because God is my strength, and He is going to do something to my feet!"

He said, "In the midst of the most controversial circumstances, God is going to make my feet like hinds' feet. My fig tree's going to blossom again; my vines are going to bear fruit again; my fields are going to yield; my flock is going to come in; and things are going to turn around for me. Why? Because I didn't look to things or circumstances for my strength.

"God is my strength. He puts His power in my feet. He puts His power in my heart. As long as I have the heart of a warrior and the feet of a runner, I will win this race — *living on the cutting edge!*"

ABOUT THE AUTHOR

Dr. Christian Harfouche is both an apostle and a prophet to the nations. Having received a divine mandate to mobilize the army of God, Dr. Harfouche has invested over 25 years in training a generation of miracle workers. Through the Word of God and the move of the Spirit, Dr. Harfouche is launching everyday believers into prophetic destiny. As a team, Drs. Christian and Robin Harfouche have ignited hearts and blazed a trail of revival across America and throughout the world. Their sincerity, genuine love and fervent commitment to global revival has inspired multitudes to answer the call of God.

Drs. Christian and Robin Harfouche are committed to training New Testament disciples at The World Center in Pensacola, Florida. The World Center is home to both the International Miracle Institute Bible Training Center and a vibrant, multi-cultural, cross-denominational church. People from around the world move to Pensacola for training and impartation from a major miracle ministry. Drs. Christian and Robin Harfouche continue to travel worldwide, conducting Miracle Soul-Winning Crusades and imparting their lives to the Body of Christ. Their influence and the miracle testimonies of their disciples can be seen daily on the highly acclaimed television program, *Miracles Today*.

International Miracle Institute (IMI)
Equipping A Generation Of Miracle–Workers!

The Lord has given Drs. Christian and Robin Harfouche a mandate to train and equip over 400,000 miracle–workers for the great end–time harvest of souls.

Through the integrity of the Word of God and the move of the Spirit, IMI is empowering a generation to live in victory and to walk in power.

Invest yourself in a supernatural training program.

Allow revelation from the Word of God and impartation from a major miracle ministry to supernaturally equip you for your end–time purpose!

IMI offers two training options!

IMI In-Residence Training (Pensacola, Florida)
IMI Correspondence Program (home study program)

IMI Training At A Glance

- Receive training by Drs. Christian and Robin Harfouche.
- Grow in a practical revelatory understanding of the Word of God.
- Learn how to have continual supernatural results in God.
- Impact the world with signs, wonders and miracles following.
- Fully accredited to confer both undergraduate and graduate degrees.

For More Information:
Visit: www.globalrevival.com
Email: IMI@globalrevival.com
Phone: 850-439-6225

Year One of IMI powerfully equips those called to walk on the cutting edge in the Word of God. This foundation enables you as a believer to live and operate in the supernatural and fulfill the call of God on your life. **Year One is an accredited year of bible college, containing over 100 hours of teaching on 96 CD's.**

Your Authority:
Become all that you can be by knowing, understanding, and exercising your authority in Jesus Christ.

Heavenly Identity:
Understand your identity in Christ.

The God Man:
Learn all about the unlimited abilities invested in you.

Great Faith:
Find out how you can grow to be a wonder worker by building your faith in God.

The Anointing:
Find out about the Anointing in you and how you can cooperate with this unction.

Miracles:
Step into a place in the Lord where nothing is impossible.

Year Two of IMI contiues where Year One left off, helping you unlock the deep truths and revelation in the Word of God. Building on the foundation of Year One, **Year Two further enables you as a believer to live and operate in the supernatural** and fulfill the call of God on your life. **Year Two is an accredited year of bible college, also containing over 100 hours of teaching on 96 CD's.**

Advanced Studies in Faith:
A study to build your faith from level to level.

Understanding the Supernatural:
Learn to operate in the highest dimension of life in the spirit.

Healing in the Atonement:
Understand your divine right to the provision and benefits of healing in the atonement.

Ministry Gifts:
"And God gave gifts unto men…" A study of the Call-The Office.

Prophets and Prophecy:
A study of Old and New Testament Prophets; recognize the spirit of error, develop the spirit of pioneer, study the predictive future Word, and learn to cooperate with the Anointing.

Demons & Demonology:
Understand the origin, operation, strategies, and the believers' dominion over the powers of darkness.

Remember, miracles don't just happen. By the Word of God and the power of the Spirit, the IMI Correspondence Program will train and equip you to be a miracle worker for this end-time harvest of souls.

"Study to show yourself approved unto God, a workman that needs not to be ashamed, rightly dividing the Word of Truth." 2 Timothy 2:15

For More Information:
Visit: www.globalrevival.com
Email: IMI@globalrevival.com
Phone: 850–439–6225

**For additional teaching resources
by Dr. Christian Harfouche
please visit us on the web at www.globalrevival.com**

or contact:

Global Revival Distribution
421 North Palafox St., Pensacola, Florida 32501
Email: info@globalrevival.com
Order Line: 850–439–9750

Real people living extraordinary lives – Miracle's Today celebrates the voice of the disciple. Televised daily around the world, Miracles Today captures the passion and purpose of a generation with a divine mandate. Embracing the promises of God and the triumphant walk of faith, Miracle's Today is the celebration of unscripted victories and real life miracle testimonies. Trained and mentored by Drs. Christian and Robin Harfouche, these disciples have answered a global call to broadcast the creative expression of God throughout the Earth. Miracle's Today is God's method of stirring a generation into destiny.

For broadcast times and stations, please visit:

www.globalrevival.com

For further information:
Christian Harfouche Ministries
421 N. Palafox St. • Pensacola, FL 32501

Office: 850–439–6225

Website: www.globalrevival.com
Email: info@globalrevival.com

For prayer: 1–86–Miracle–4
prayer@globalrevival.com